WILLIAM MORRIS

DESIGNS AND PATTERNS

INTRODUCTION BY
NORAH C. GILLOW

KEEPER, WILLIAM MORRIS GALLERY, LONDON

CRESCENT BOOKS
NEW YORK

THIS EDITION PUBLISHED BY CRESCENT BOOKS,
DISTRIBUTED BY CROWN PUBLISHERS, Inc., 225 PARK AVENUE SOUTH,
NEW YORK, NEW YORK 10003.

WILLIAM MORRIS DESIGNS AND PATTERNS
IS A REPRESENTATIVE SELECTION OF MATERIAL FROM
THE WILLIAM MORRIS GALLERY
LLOYD PARK, FOREST ROAD
LONDON E17 4PP
ENGLAND

POSTER ART SERIES

WILLIAM MORRIS DESIGNS AND PATTERNS
IS A VOLUME IN THE POSTER ART
SERIES. UP TO TEN PLATES MAY BE
REPRODUCED IN ANY ONE PROJECT OR
PUBLICATION, WITHOUT SPECIAL PERMISSION
AND FREE OF CHARGE. WHEREVER POSSIBLE THE
AUTHOR, TITLE AND PUBLISHER SHOULD BE ACKNOWLEDGED
IN A CREDIT NOTE. FOR PERMISSION TO MAKE MORE EXTENSIVE USE
OF THE PLATES IN THIS BOOK APPLICATION
MUST BE MADE TO THE PUBLISHER.

ISBN 0 517 66116 0

PRINTED AND BOUND IN ITALY

h g f e d c b a

INTRODUCTION

When William Morris died in 1896, an eminent physician remarked that though specific ailments had been the immediate cause of death, the disease which killed him was 'simply being William Morris, and having done more than most ten men' – a comment which sums up both the multiplicity of his talents and the extraordinary energy with which he pursued a number of careers, all within a lifetime of little more than sixty years.

As a designer, his ideas were embodied in the work of the firm he founded, Morris and Co., which produced stained glass, ceramics, metalwork, furniture, wallpapers and textiles. He also embarked upon a 'little typographical adventure' printing fine books at his Kelmscott Press and delivered lectures on art and socialism which influenced successive generations of designers and craftsmen. As a poet and writer his work received critical acclaim and had a wide readership. He wrote *The Defence of Guenevere* in a medieval vein, composed *The Earthly Paradise* as a narrative epic, and explored many styles and literary forms including Norse saga and prose romance.

Fundamental to these activities was the belief that art and society are inextricably linked – 'art' for Morris meaning not only the fine arts of painting and sculpture, but 'that great body of art by means of which men have at all times . . . striven to beautify the familiar matter of everyday life.' He believed that such art arose from a basic human instinct to create, and was 'a joy to the maker and user alike' in that it satisfied personal creative talent and at the same time enriched society as a whole. But the traditions upon which such art rested – the skills of the artist-craftsman, which Morris saw exemplified in medieval workshop practice and the guild system – had been eroded. Since the Renaissance the concept of the artist as a unique and special genius had led to a diminution in status of the craftsman and an inevitable division between the fine and decorative arts. This distinction had a particularly adverse effect on applied art, especially during the eighteenth century when the rise of an affluent middle class led to an increased demand for furniture and furnishings.

The gradual introduction of mechanization, enabled faster, cheaper production, in quantity and to a standardized uniformity – factors which meant that the individual was no longer required to know all parts of a process providing one part could be repeated competently, nor to develop and contribute personal creative skills. Mass production and mechanization necessitated the reorganization of the workforce under the factory system. This led in turn to the growth of industrialization, and appalling social conditions for those who laboured to produce wealth but were given little share of it. For Morris, the Industrial Revolution had produced a society which denied to the mass of its members the means and opportunity both of creative work and quality of life. These fundamental rights, he believed, could only be restored by an equally radical reorganization through socialism. This would bring about a society in which the public, having control of all resources, would have the power to decide how these could best be used for the good of all.

Morris's commitment to socialism in the 1880s was the outcome of trends evident much earlier in his life. The problems he encountered during his career as a designer led him inexorably to the conclusion that the attempt to reform art was useless unless accompanied by fundamental changes in society. The extent of the crisis in the applied arts was first brought home to him in practical terms when attempting to furnish Red House, the home built for him by Philip Webb. Unable to find suitable furniture or furnishings, Morris and a group of friends undertook the task themselves – a project which gave rise to the foundation of Morris & Co. in 1861. Attempts to reform and improve design in previous decades, where the revival of decorative art had been seen mainly in terms of industrial manufacture had meant the artist supplying designs to be executed by others, usually by factory mass production. The partners in Morris & Co., however, considered themselves to be 'Fine Art Workmen' and took as their model the artist-craftsman, who both designed and carried out his work. This remained the guiding principle of the firm, even when expansion of business meant that production had to be delegated to others. Morris himself insisted on mastering the techniques, processes and materials involved in the various media for which he designed, and on taking as active a role as possible in production.

His pre-eminence as a pattern designer rested on certain basic principles, evident in his work and summarized in his lectures on the subject. Structure was a crucial element of pattern designing, providing, in Morris's words, 'a wall against vagueness' by means of 'definite form bounded by firm outline'. In his lecture, *Some Hints on Pattern Designing*, 1881, he traced the history of repeating patterns from ancient and classical times to the Gothic period in which a significant change in pattern structure took place, marked by what he called 'the universal acceptance of continuous growth'. This was based either on 'the branch formed on a diagonal line' or 'the net framed on variously-proportioned diamonds' – structures which, with variations, were the basis for Morris's own patterns. As he pointed out in his lectures, Nature was an obvious source of inspiration, not to be copied literally, but to be imitated in its 'natural forms which are at once most familiar and most delightful to us, as well from association as from beauty.' This power of evocation and suggestion was what gave patterns their 'meaning'. 'You may be sure', wrote Morris, 'that any decoration is futile . . . when it does not remind you of something beyond itself, of something of which it is but a visible symbol.'

Morris's first wallpapers were designed in the early 1860s, among them *Trellis* and *Daisy*, both of which have noticeably geometric pattern structures. In the case of *Trellis* (plates 2a, 2b), the structure is based on a grid of horizontals and verticals, and in *Daisy* (plate 1), on horizontal bands formed by the two alternating rows of clumps of flowers. After several unsatisfactory attempts to print these wallpapers himself, using etched zinc plates and transparent colours, Morris approached Jeffrey & Co., of Islington, a reputable firm which from 1864 undertook the printing. The designs were traced onto pearwood blocks which were then cut and the papers printed using distemper colours. These early wallpapers each required twelve blocks to print the complete pattern and were thus expensive to produce at a time when the firm's finances were limited and commissions for domestic decoration scarce. Apart from a few monochrome papers dating from the late 1860s, some of which were adaptations of traditional designs, it was not until the early 1870s that Morris turned again to designing wallpapers. Most of these were based on meandering lines flowing across the surface in a loose informal pattern which deliberately concealed the structure of the repeats. The effect, in wallpapers such as *Larkspur* (plate 3) and *Willow* (plate 4) was of spontaneous growth, freshness and naturalism. In others, such as *Chrysanthemum* (plate 6), the major elements of the pattern – the flower-heads, leaves and stems – were superimposed on a secondary network of tiny fronds, enlivening the whole surface and creating the illusion of shallow depth. Similar spatial effects were achieved in *Acanthus* (plate 5) with its pattern of leaves undulating in scrolls, winding and weaving up the wallpaper, their volume being accentuated by a subtle gradation of colour for which sixteen blocks were required.

By 1876, Morris's interest in weaving led him to introduce a more rigid, formalized framework into his designs, many of which were based on a vertical turn-over structure adopted from weaving patterns. Naturalistic elements became more conventionalized, and instead of flowing across the surface, flowers and leaves were trained to fit shapes – scrolls, as in *Pimpernel* (plate 7), or ogees and ovals, as in *Sunflower*. Morris's study of historic textiles at this period, particularly the collections at the South Kensington Museum (now the Victoria & Albert Museum) had a distinct influence on his own pattern designs. Indeed, the marked diagonal emphasis characteristic of so many patterns from 1883 to 1890 – both in wallpapers and in printed chintzes such as *Wey*, *Evenlode* and *Wandle* (plates 20, 21, 26) – almost certainly derived from the similar design structure of a fine piece of Italian cut velvet which the Museum acquired in 1883.

The last period, from 1890 to 1896, saw a return to more flowing, less rigid patterns, often with an upward movement swaying from side to side. Some late wallpapers, such as *Blackthorn* (plate 11) used the same range of naturalistic elements as the early wallpapers – daisies, fritillaries, violets and blackthorn sprays – but carefully arranged in a symmetrical structure, combining formal design with a loose bower-like effect.

As a pattern designer, it was not long before Morris turned his attention to textiles, but here he encountered difficulties in production. By the late 1860s, traditional methods of hand-block printing using dyes made from vegetable and organic substances had been replaced almost entirely in commercial manufacture by the quicker, cheaper methods of machine printing with engraved rollers using chemical dyes, chiefly aniline dyes derived from coal tar. Although easier to prepare and use than traditional dyes, chemical dyes had distinct disadvantages; – the colours tended to be harsh and garish, and not only faded rapidly but unevenly – thus producing distortions in the pattern. A few textile printers still used hand-block printing to a limited extent and it was to one such commercial firm, Thomas Clarkson & Co., near Preston, that Morris turned for the printing of his first fabrics. The result was unsatisfactory, and he next approached Thomas Wardle, an expert on dyeing techniques and the history and processes of silk production. It was at Wardle's works at Leek in Staffordshire that the sixteen chintzes which Morris designed between 1875 and 1880 were printed, before he acquired his own workshops at Merton Abbey, Surrey. In addition to the help and advice of Wardle, Morris consulted a variety of sources, including medieval herbals, to discover recipes for the old dyes, and by experimentation finally managed to produce a satisfactory range of colours; red from madder and various insect substances, yellow from weld and different barks, brown from walnut tree roots and walnut husks, and blue from woad and indigo. From these he built up a range of soft, clear colours, subtle in tone, blending together harmoniously, and stable when exposed to light. He described his use of 'frank reds and blues . . . the mainstays of the colour arrangements . . . softened by the paler shades of red, outlined in black and made more tender by the addition of yellow in small quantities, mostly forming part of brightish greens.'

One of the traditional methods which Morris revived was that of discharge-printing; madder and indigo were the two dyes he particularly favoured for this process. Instead of printing colours onto a plain cloth, as in surface printing, in the discharge method, entire bolts of cloth were first dyed to a uniform shade in the vats, the pattern then being made by using various strengths of bleaching re-agents. Where a strong solution was used, as in the case of *Bird and Anemone* chintz (plate 18) the background colour (madder/red) was completely removed from the cloth, leaving a white pattern. A weaker solution made the pattern appear in a half-tone on a full-colour ground, as in the *Brother Rabbit* chintz (plate 19) where the background remains a deep shade of indigo while the pattern of little rabbits is in a lighter tone. Morris experimented with variations of this discharge process, using additional colours, mainly yellow and red. Where these were superimposed over half-indigo portions in the design, delicate shades of green and pink were achieved, as in the chintzes *Kennet* (plate 23), *Wey* and *Wandle*. Occasionally, a further colour was added such as the soft brown used for the birds in *Strawberry Thief* (plate 24), a design inspired by the sight of thrushes creeping under the fruit nets in the garden at Kelmscott Manor, Morris's country retreat in Oxfordshire.

Morris's designs for woven textiles were, on the whole, more obviously influenced by his study of medieval and later hand-woven fabrics. For instance, the patterns in woven wool such as *Peacock and Dragon* (plate 30) and *Bird* (plate 31) bear close resemblance to pieces in the South Kensington Museum's collection of historic textiles. At first, most of Morris's woven fabrics were produced by outside companies, but in 1877, he installed a Jacquard loom in a workshop near the firm's Queen Square premises and brought over a silk weaver from Lyons, one of the great silk-weaving centres of Europe. Later, when he acquired premises at Merton Abbey, there was space to develop his own weaving workshops, though some fabrics continued to be woven by other firms.

Weaving, by the very nature of its technique, presented endless possibilities for creating textural effects which Morris exploited to the full in his designs. In damask, such as *St. James* (plate 33), by using tone on tone of the same soft rose colour he created a sense of depth. In *Golden Bough* (plate 34), the use of different types of yarn achieved a contrast between the shimmering gold and green silks of the main element of the design and the duller surface of the linen background. In *Dove and Rose* (plate 32) this use of different yarns was combined with a complicated triple-weave technique, in which parts of the silk tissue stand out in relief from the fine wool background, giving a rich and varied surface effect.

Given his love of Persian and oriental carpets of which he owned several splendid examples, it is hardly surprising that Morris also began to design rugs and carpets. Some, such as the *Lily* Wilton pile carpet (plate 35) were machine-woven by outside firms, while others were handmade on looms set up in the coach-house adjoining Kelmscott House, his Hammersmith home. These smaller 'Hammersmith' rugs (plate 36) were available at the firm's showrooms at 449 Oxford Street, but the full-size carpets were made to order, their patterns being named after the houses for which they were originally commissioned. Morris maintained that the pattern in carpet design should be 'quite flat, that it should give no more at least than the merest hint of one plane behind another' to avoid the uncomfortable feeling of walking over a surface which simulated high relief. He believed that 'every little bit of surface must have its own individual beauty of material and colour', as indeed was the case in the eastern tradition of carpet design.

It was at Kelmscott House that Morris wove his first experimental piece of tapestry on a high-warp loom – a technique which had almost died out in Britain. Thereafter he taught his craftsmen the process and the firm produced various tapestries at Merton Abbey, in most cases with single figures designed by Edward Burne-Jones (a close friend and original partner in the firm), and foliage backgrounds by Morris or his chief assistant, J. H. Dearle. In reviving the technique, Morris returned to the principles of medieval tapestry design; using decoration rather than elaborate pictorial effects and introducing scrolls inscribed with verses in Gothic lettering. *The Woodpecker* (plate 38), a high-warp tapestry and the unique example of this subject was designed by Morris in about 1885 and woven at Merton Abbey. It exemplifies Morris's view of the qualities of tapestry in its combination of flat decoration with shallow depth in the main subject. Scrolling acanthus leaves wind around the trunk of the tree with its brightly coloured fruit and bird, framed by a border of honeysuckle climbing around poles. Above and below, verses describe the theme: 'I once a king and chief, now am the tree-bark's thief, ever 'twixt trunk and leaf chasing the prey'. The poem, composed by Morris, refers to the legend of Picus, an ancient Italian king who was turned into a woodpecker (in Latin 'picus') by the enchantress Circe as a punishment for his refusal to succumb to her advances.

Embroidery also formed an important part of the firm's work and was an art in which Morris had a special interest. Indeed, the embroideries which he and his wife Jane worked for Red House, from the simple *Daisy* hangings to the more ambitious series of figure panels, were pioneer efforts in the revival of traditional embroidery techniques. Morris's younger daughter May (1862–1938) took over much of the designing and organization of the firm's embroidery section and her accomplishments as a needlewoman can be seen in the cushion cover which she worked in silks and gold thread, to Morris's design, *The Flowerpot* (plate 40). Apart from ecclesiastical work, the firm produced a wide range of items for domestic use, either made to order or which clients could make themselves by purchasing pieces of fabric ready stencilled with patterns, together with dyed silks, wools and gold thread. Frequently the firm would receive commissions for larger, more elaborate pieces, such as *The Artichoke* (plate 39), one of a series of panels worked by Mrs. Ada Godman from a design by Morris. This panel in crewel wools on a natural cotton twill ground is a fine example of the range of subtle shades and colour harmonies achieved by the use of indigo, madder and other organic dyes.

In this brief survey of Morris's work, perhaps the last word on his ideas and ideals in the decorative arts should be left to Morris himself: 'We ought to get to understand the value of intelligent work, the work of men's hands guided by their brains, and to take that, though it may be rough, rather than the unintelligent work of machines or slaves, though it be delicate; to refuse altogether to use machine-made work unless where the nature of the thing made compels it, or where the machine does what mere human suffering would otherwise have to do; to have a high standard of excellence in wares and not to accept makeshifts for the real thing, but rather to go without; to have no ornament merely for fashion's sake, but only because we really think it beautiful . . .'

NORAH C. GILLOW,
KEEPER, WILLIAM MORRIS GALLERY, LONDON
NOVEMBER 1987

PLATE 1

Daisy Wallpaper, 1864

*Horizontal bands are formed in the pattern
by two alternating rows of clumps of
flowers*

PLATE 3
Larkspur Wallpaper, 1872
This plate shows the polychrome version of
1874

PLATE 4

Willow Wallpaper, 1874

This pattern develops the effect of spontaneous growth, freshness and naturalism which Morris had begun to explore in Larkspur (plate 3)

PLATE 6

Chrysanthemum Wallpaper, 1876 (Design)

In this design the major elements of the pattern – the flower-heads, leaves and stems – are superimposed on a secondary network of tiny fronds which enlivens the whole surface and creates an illusion of shallow depth

PLATE 12
Tulip Chintz, 1875

PLATE 15
Indian Diaper Chintz, 1876

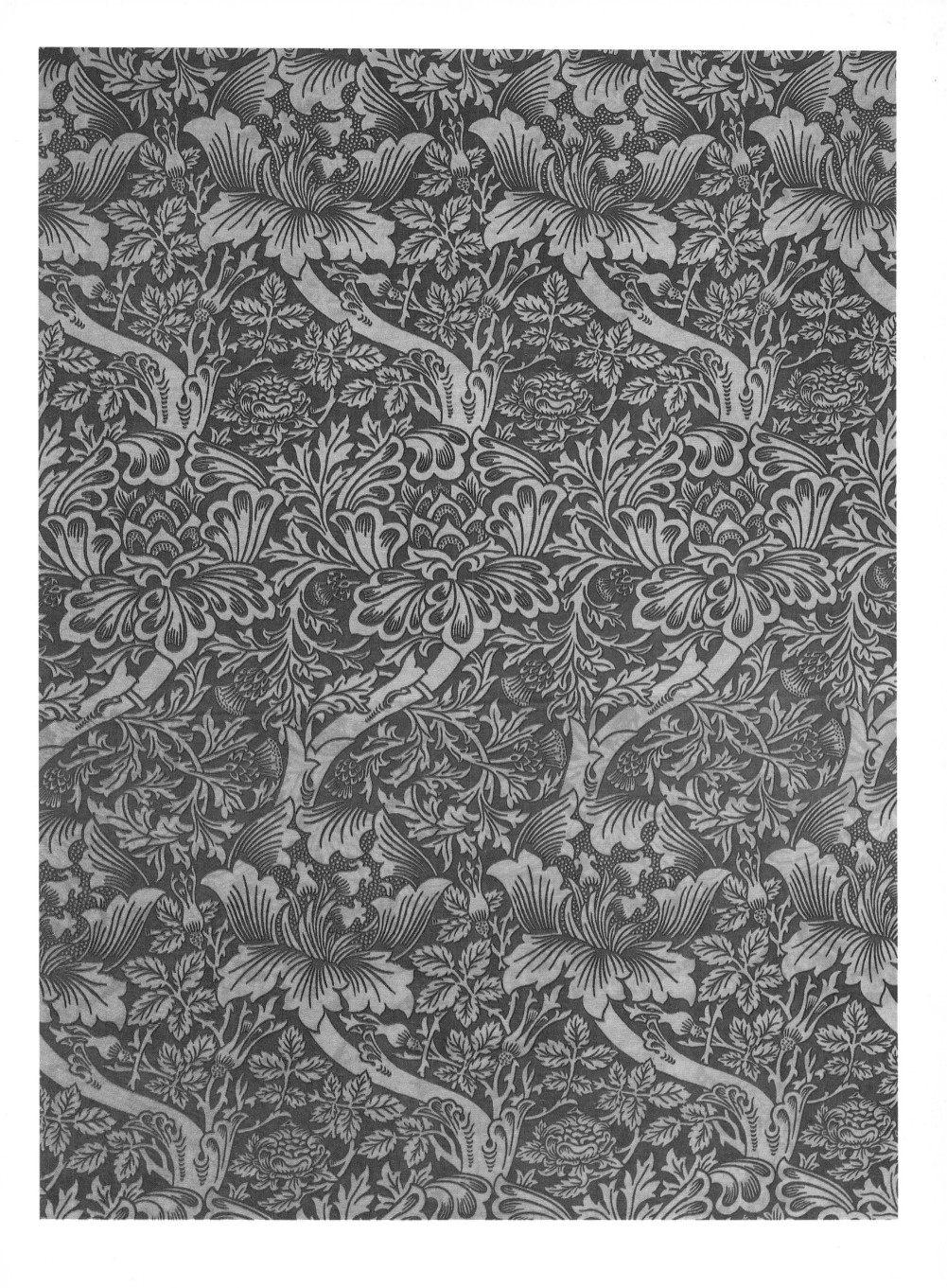

PLATE 17
Rose and Thistle Chintz, 1881

PLATE 18

Bird and Anemone Chintz, 1881–1882

Morris produced this fabric using the traditional method of discharge-printing. Instead of printing colours onto a plain cloth as in surface printing, entire bolts of cloth were first dyed to a uniform shade in the vats, the pattern then being made by using various strengths of bleaching re-agents. Where a strong solution was used, the background colour would be completely removed from the cloth, leaving a white pattern

PLATE 20

Wey Chintz, 1883

This printed chintz almost certainly derives its design structure from a fine piece of Italian cut velvet which Morris saw in the South Kensington Museum (now the Victoria and Albert Museum)

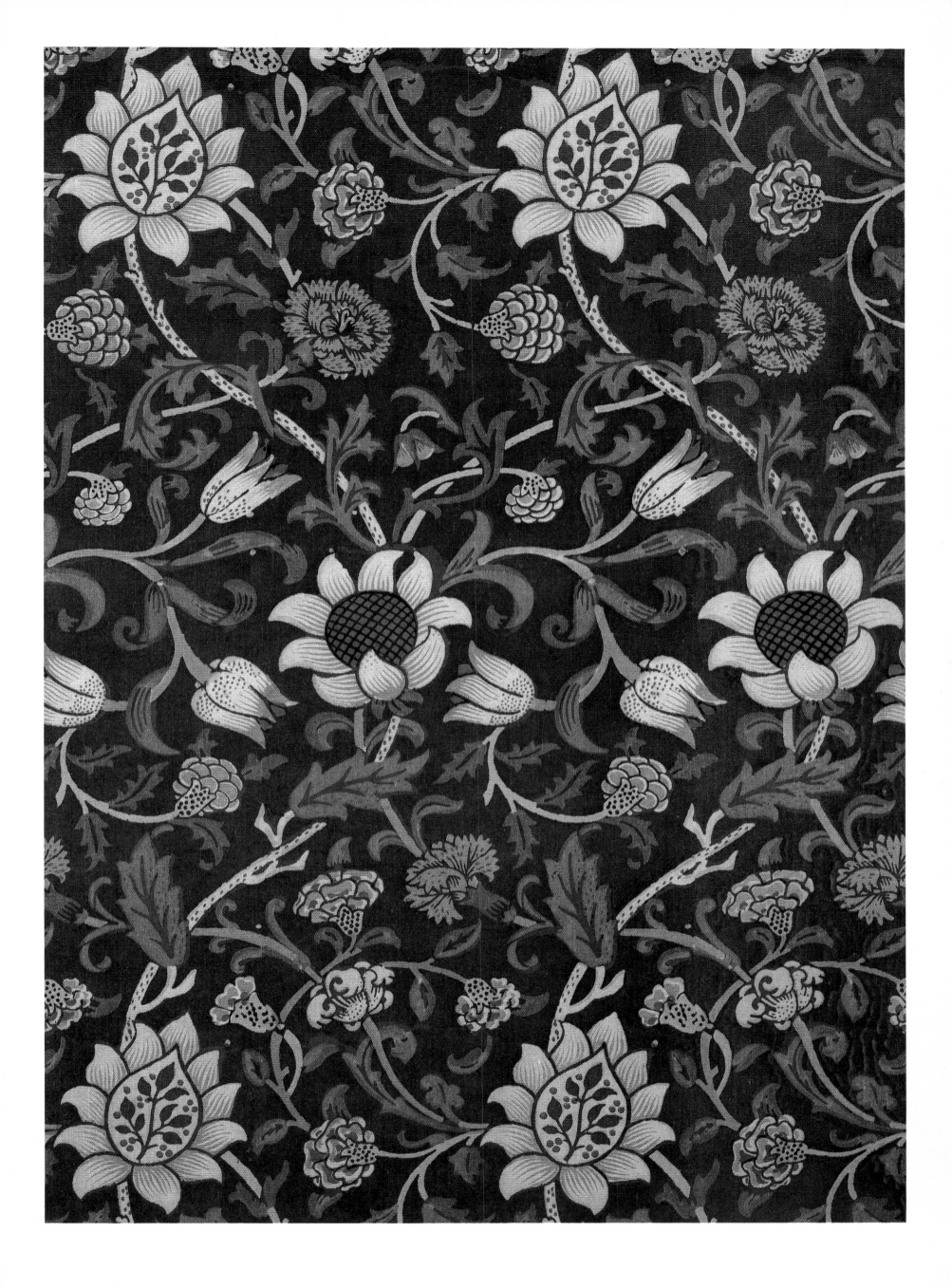

PLATE 22
Rose Chintz, 1883

PLATE 27
Lodden Chintz, 1884

PLATE 28
Medway Chintz, 1885

PLATE 29
Honeycomb Woven Wool, 1876

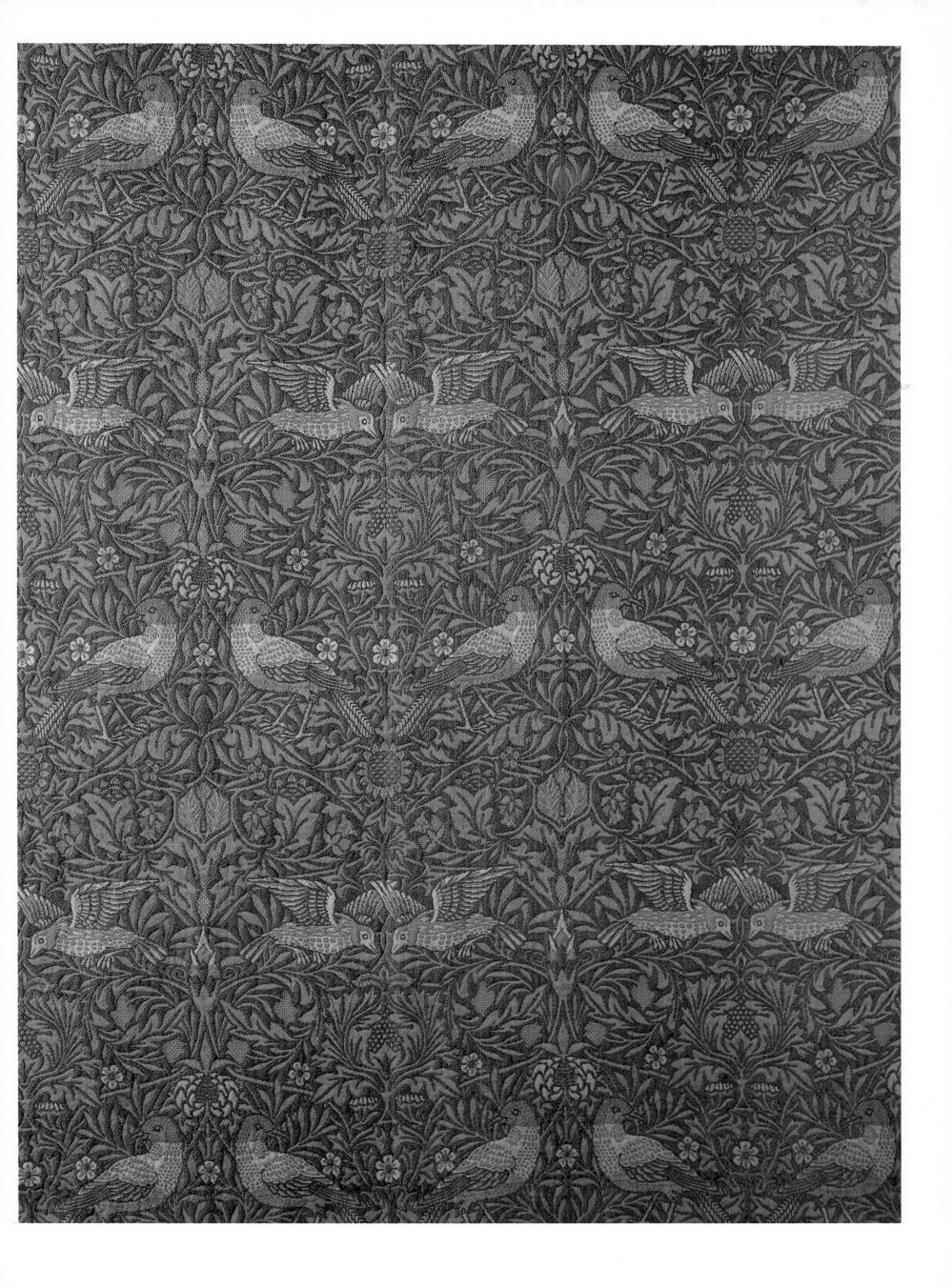

PLATE 31
Bird Woven Wool, 1878

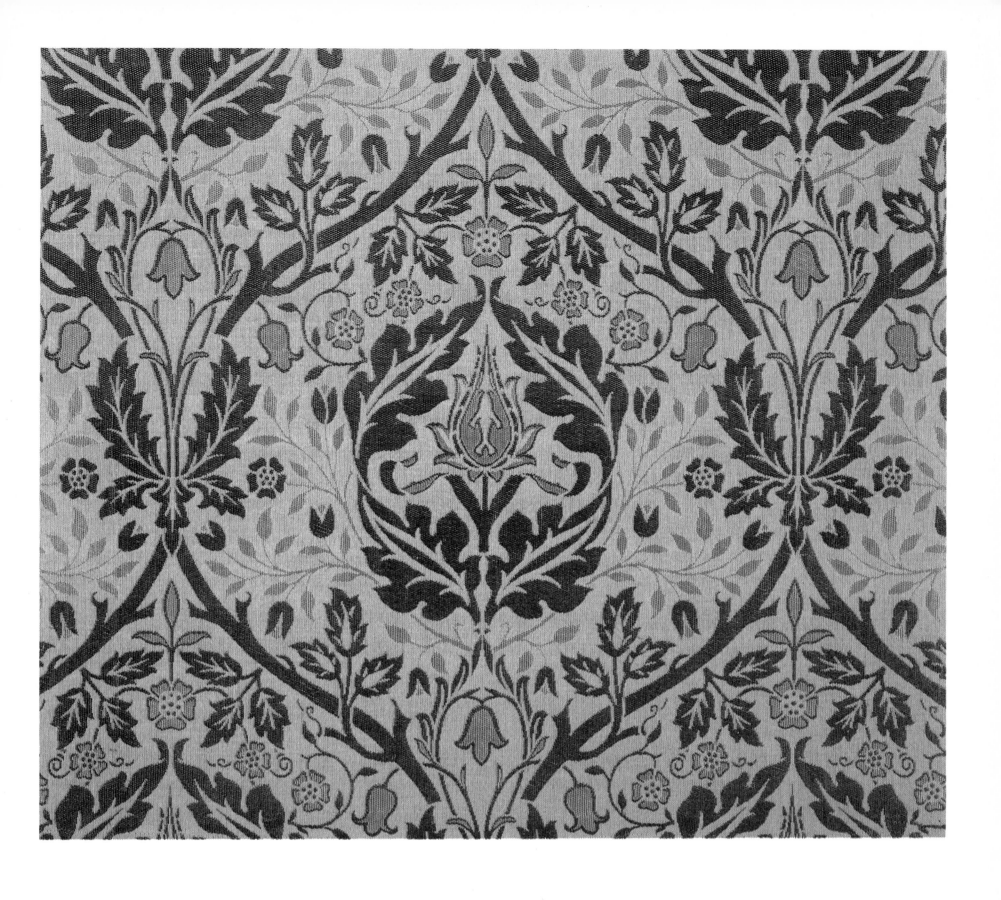

PLATE 34

Golden Bough Woven Textile, 1888

By using different types of yarn, Morris achieves a contrast between the shimmering gold and green silks of the main element of the design and the duller surface of the linen background

PLATE 35

Lily Wilton Pile Carpet, 1875

Given his love of Persian and oriental carpets of which he owned several splendid examples, it is hardly surprising that Morris also began to design rugs and carpets. This example was machine woven by an outside firm although others were hand-made on looms by Morris and Co., (see plate 36)

PLATE 36

Hammersmith Rug, circa 1890

*This example was woven on a hand loom
at Merton Abbey in the manner of those
rugs which were produced in the coach house
adjoining Morris's Hammersmith home,
Kelmscott House. These small "Hammersmith Rugs" were available at the firm's
showrooms at 449 Oxford Street*

PLATE 37

Tile Panel, 1887

*This panel was designed by William Morris
and made by William de Morgan*

i once a king and chief · now am the tree-barks thief :

ever twixt trunk and leaf · chasing the prey · ·

The Woodpecker Tapestry, circa 1885

*This example produced on a high-warp loom
exemplifies Morris's view of the qualities of
tapestry in its combination of flat decoration
with shallow depth in the main subject.
Scrolling acanthus leaves wind round the
trunk of the tree with its brightly coloured
fruit and bird, framed by a border of honeysuckle climbing around poles. Above and
below are lines from a poem by Morris based
on the legend of Picus, an ancient Italian
king who was turned into a woodpecker*

PLATE 39

The Artichoke Panel, 1877

Frequently Morris and Co. would receive commissions for elaborate pieces of embroidery. This panel is one of a series worked by Mrs. Ada Godman from a design by Morris. The panel is in crewel wools on a natural cotton twill ground, and is a fine example of the range of subtle shades and colour harmonies achieved by the use of organic rather than chemical dyes

PLATE 40

The Flower Pot Embroidered Cushion Cover
1880

Morris's younger daughter May (1862–
1938) took over much of the designing and
organization of Morris and Co.'s embroidery
section, and her accomplishments as a needle-
woman are exemplified in this cushion cover
which she worked in silk and gold thread to
her father's design